Creation and Other Poems

Creation and Other Poems

By

Ekkehard-Teja Wilke.

ISBN:	Softcover	978-1-7960-2212-4
	eBook	978-1-7960-2213-1

Print information available on the last page.

Rev. date: 03/15/2019

To order additional copies of this book, contact:
Xlibris
1-888-795-4274
www.Xlibris.com
Orders@Xlibris.com
793276

Table of Contents

For Kiri and Marc

Haesi

CREATION

21 November:
Happy birthday, Latrice

As like a grain of sand on the beach
As like an ear of wheat in the fields
Countless
We are
And easily well within reach

The way
and yet, as one
and always everywhere
unbound Prometheus at bay

defining you
by what you are, not ever what you do -
as form and substance
in context of our world

If when you do call, shall
Arrive,
reach out to us who know.
We do project our image:
bold, stark, and tall, - and live
which now be also you,
And thus you shall survive

By choice, by fate we are your mirror
We reflect
And thus we too are
You.
Now, ever.

Become, commit
to who you are
And then
You will
          but
          Live

Then but you will become.
You Are

HALLOWEEN

Linda, 17 Nov 2006:
Happy birthday

Cat Woman
Wild thing
On Halloween Day
You are wearing my ring

Cat Woman
Center stage
On Halloween Night:
Frenzy and Fright

Cat Woman
Cold, Broken, Alone
Post Halloween
And I carry you home

Cat Woman
Long gone day:
Halloweens pass
Memories stay

TO MY SISTERS

For Br, Ch, and Si, 2006

Brianna, Leeza, Danielle:

And of course, you speak logic and truth
You speak of loneliness, of pain,
You speak of injustice, of hate,
Of rights denied, opportunities withdrawn,
You speak of happiness destroyed

You say: I want to better myself
You say: I want to quit
You say – but sometimes -
you are just silent

And I say: I am concerned, you are a part of me – you are my sister

Of course you are right –
You say: supply and demand
You say: balance the checkbook
You say – but sometimes -
you are just silent.

And I say: I care for you; you are a part of me - you are my sister

Of course you are right:
You say: oh, well, the guys –
You say: I bracket out and think of benefits
You say – but sometimes –
you speak just silence

and then I say: I love you –
and leave it just at that

Of course you are right-
You say: And anyway, what's it to You?"
Control?, aggression? An egotrip?
A fantasy of rape, condoned 'cause paid for in advance?
You say: some brute getting his kicks at my expense?
Taking advantage of power and privilege
(but then: what should I care!)
You say – but sometimes then -you merely –
smile
("I am available… "I can't wait… "Let me be…. ")
and act the willing servant
cross city and county,
cross country and state,
cross ocean and continent:

Whiting, Vegas, Versailles
Cash for Service!!?

I

I bracket the world and change the moment to eternity.
You block the hour and transform the object of relief into your visions of your benefits,
Perhaps, or visions of
rage, revenge
- retaliation?

Of course you are right:
You ask:
Who shares with me the Prayer of the Lord?
Who gives me shelter?

        Who pays my bills?
Who gives me food?
        Who gives?
Who cares?:
        Who does?
Who?
        Who?

                Tell me:
                        Is it
        My brother? (perhaps: later)
        My sister? (perhaps: never)
        My father? (perhaps: who?)
        My mother (Perhaps: I wish I could)

                        Is it
                My neighbor? (Perhaps: have you no respect?)
                My church? (perhaps: have you no faith?)
                My teacher? (Perhaps: have you not learned?)

                        Is it
        My city? (pay fines pay taxes)
        My state? (Pay dues pay taxes)
        My country? (Pay up, put up, shut up)

                        Is it?
        Well: Is It??

II

I answer you now when I now tell you now that I am of one of those

who brought cruelty and death
        (but who also knew how to die)

who flung fire and terror
(but who also affirmed their fate)
who thrust torture and devastation onto black-red, brown-golden lands,
onto vast gray-white fields of snow,
unfathomable blue-green depths of water,
azure-steel-gray infinities of sky
(and who, scorning redemption, destroyed their souls - and crippled ours).

And now,
survivor in quest of re-pair and re-legion,
in quest of the Blue Flower sprung from the wounds of fragmentation
I re-cognize you as my sister, as a part of myself.

You are in my home always open and welcome.
In my thoughts cared and engaged.
In my heart loved and retained.
And my humanity for ever will hold you in embrace

III

Why, do you ask: why Me?

Why?
Well just because:
Because you are beautiful and black and brave;
Because you are compassionate and strong and proud;
Because you are radiant and resourceful and real;
Because -
Well, just because,
Because you are the You who Is –
That's Why

Strong through humiliation,
Resilient through injustice,
Compassionate through discrimination,
Wise through suffering,
You carry the vision, the will, and the voice.
You shoulder the weight, preserve the dignity, and harbor the source of love.
[did you not tell me: I am a good person?
Did you not say: I have a great personality?
Did you not mention: I love horses?]

So then now tell me:
What can you gain, how can I give, what you already have?
How can you lose, what can I take, from what you never had?
Ever give what you will never miss
Ever take what you will never know
ever give always take never?

My eyes perceive your tears and see the sparkling diamonds;
My ears receive your lamentations and hear the testament of joy;
My touch conceives your presence, the harbinger of peace.

We are the ones who were
You were the ones we are

NO I AM NOT

For, you, Sidney: 29 May 06
happy birthday

No, I am not the river Niger -

But I am and

I saw you
molded from ribbed clay;

I saw you
dancing the Garden of Eden toward the Tree of the Snake;

I saw you
walking harsh and unforgiving lands;

I saw you
weary and torn (Nivea the magician);

I saw you
carrying faith and hope in the image of mystery.

And now -

I am and I be

and I shall await your return

WESSON- SMITH

take care, DCRBQ: have a good new year.

To reckon with!:
Wesson and Smith
Smith- Wesson
We learned our lesson
from now on no more to beg for a coke
No more the shuffle, no more the butt of a joke
To you, Bertie: First comes Smith-Wesson,
No more the stooge for some two-bit no-good con
(indeed we Have learned That lesson)
pride and respect, esteem - an ego trip to Baal
and then and only then,(erst dann)
Erst kommt das Fressen – und dann erst dann kommt die Moral
First comes the grub and then, and only then, morality, Moral

The deed - indeed:
A cool show – a marvelous feat
Respect on the street
Chicks, acting heat, sweet, tricks, cheap
Cheat in their heads, inside of cars, in alley corners, and on their feet
We play them pigs and the fuzz on the beat
Cops and robbers – endless repeat of advance and retreat
Nervy, high-risk, but
Neat
Today we are somebody.
Not just some body!

Kick high, fly wild,
chase clouds and dreams
like the carefree innocent child
we once were it seems --

Touch every star
	Nightbright, and visible in a cool-blue sky
Bacause we ARE
	But:
And tomorrow we DIE
(Stacy: It all good. Stacy: No. Stacy, Stacy: Why?)

Blown off our feet –
	now leave us alone, now let us be!:
Gutters, sides of the street,
defiled creations.
deferred dreams
Lonely places,
contested spaces
choked screams –
tarped under Canvas
Contorted, dead, ashen faces

	Foreseen, foretold, but all the same unbidden
All that we now once were:
Inheritance to Life, the living.
And busy omnipresent ghoulish mites
Cold and relentless under revolving artificial lights
Report in detail bit by gory bit
to their world all the what, the how, the why,
as they but only they see fit.
	Foreseen, foretold, unbidden

loves and burdens all once borne –
	now inventoried, sanitized,
	highlit by flashing lights
			then carried off, boxed in, and hidden
	Foreseen, foretold, but all the same unbidden

We have reclaimed the stronghold,
	Power

Re-entered the free unconquered guarded tower

Wenn wir Toten erwachen! Werdet ihr lebend nicht lange mehr lachen!
[[when we, the dead, awake, alive you will not laugh much longer]]

Pale cousins, oh had you never been
Would then have never met –
Now generations intervene –
Who keeps the measure of extracted blood and tears and sweat?

Contained, enchained, detached, re-trained
Wenn wir Toten erwachen werdet ihr Lebende nicht lange mehr lachen!
[[when we the dead awake, you Living ones will not laugh much longer]]

And by the way –
Have you had your reassurance for the day
Boosted your ego at our expense?
In our face, behind your coward fence?
With insults, nightsticks, firearms and mace?
Made you feel big, eh? You putting us back in our place?

Carlos: Recollection of memorable events!
Figures in front of a mirror
The middle passages - beginnings and ends

But no:
Masked hate
Hidden tears
Inaudible cries
Suppressed fears
Love?
We let just see

what you for us
you want, you need, for us to be
        (what we, for us,
        we want for you to see)
You dumb-struck god-forsaken fools
still you insist:" You can't fool me!":

Carved deeply into anthracitic oak
worked into calloused life-lined hands
arms calibrated, stretched, and broke
whipped into bodies disfigured by ennobled, dark- red scarred strands
bathed in red foam,
        (the horror -the humiliation)

Inherited traditions,
soul death chants hummed,
confined amongst envisioned sacrificial shrines
impressed into the brain
        (the horror -the humiliation)

seared into souls:
compressed gray-ashen hate
became and ever since has been
the source of strength:
resist, defy,
defy, retaliate,
survive.
Resist, defy; defy, survive; survive: retaliate

And Mocha, Lexus, Leslie?
Leeza, Stacy?
Leeza has chosen to become a-zeel
(she always will remain -
        Sleek still, still beautiful, high class genteel)
Stacy of course is Y cats:

why cats, turning turned backs on heel
[It all good: Stacy? [Stacy! No! For real!]

Suspects
conceiling sickles of new-moon shapes sharp as the teeth of bats
Half moons
Brown-green round wise full moon eyes
Voracious black holes in mysterious skies
Beware:
once touched, they keep you willing victim prize
Take heed, give way, be loved – take care

RAGE

for you, Sharon

I

Nothing
Nirvana
Love

Dust
Clay
Flesh

Hey hi there, Sis, Hallo!
I and You:
We have been separated since pre-birth
We two -
We All

Intoxicated with music
I dissolve my body:
    Compounds into essences, effervescent and ephemeral:
    Applied chemistry
        Elective core affinities
But only: probably not
We.
Which is
    not
to say
that we
    not
be bonded yet
some day

Generations I am and in the remoteness of time
Etched into memory and manners
Clear and ever present:
That appeal in form of a question:
Don't you believe in making people happy?

II

April, he said, be the cruelest month?
Two souls, he said, just two souls?
One hell, they say, but one hell?

III

Hey macho man: phallic fallacy
                    Phyrric victory
Hey brazen amazon: vaginal vanity
                    Maya's translucent veil
ageless endless open mystery – history's continuances – red thread, read threat

   Come cum, cunt
   ram rod, runt
      Hallo
     Immanuel

Most every female plays at hussy
Most every female trades some pussy – sometime
                    for real!-
      With a bit of tit and ass to go
      the Reader Eros dot com and Midnightchicago New City et al.
         they can tell you, they know

Most every hemale craves lush pussy
Most every hemale lusts to play - astride big butt -beneath big tit,
(showers - Meschugge - shit)
some hussy –
for real! -
sometime.
the Reader Eros dot com and Midnightchicago New City and all
they can tell you, they write, they do the storyline

come cum, cunt,
ramrod, runt
Come sea men
Come see, men
Cum semen
Come now! See! MEN
Meschugge - merde - - shit

Gwen David the huckster of hookers will pretty much
Tell you the same
(Not that his voice carries the weight of the guardian angel:
Charlie, touching the stars and talking of fairyprincesses --

Hey you, Sis, princess disguised for some as a bitch,
For others as the Virgin Mary Madonna
entrapped by a wicket Witch:
You know that, Dream Catcher Rose Bowl Queen,
how else, prey tell
dare You explain Me
Well - ?)

Come on, all, come!
Swing around the Rosie
Ten Nine Seven Five
and
Three Two One

Swing
        around the cozy ring
rosy
    the thong thing - thing thong:
     Ding dong
                [and then there were none]
        Yes, You there: Hallo!
Wake up!

IV

Medals they gave us
Heroes they called us
        - until we turned tables -:

    Now outcasts we are -
unwelcome reminders,
rejected embarrassments.
    Cripples despised,
    perverts and criminals!
        `The scum of the earth –
                Refuse
            re-fuse:
                fuse
    But just, now, you wait:
    We did.
        We bid our time.

    Now your story, now Your line
    has come –
    Your Fate:

Those who chance cross our path
            We, if we so feel, we will:

Will help – no strings attached
Will use – no quests, no compensation
And We Will Kill – (sapphire: do the wild thing?)
Still.
that is: If we so feel, we will -
to those who chance cross our path.

But
those who crossed us,
those who unleashed slaughter, bitterness, and rage
for those we do premeditate, strike with full deliberate intent
(Und morgen schlagen wir zurueck)*
On those we wage:
and do inflict the cruelest measures of revenge
And not in vain
On those who crossed us;

Numbed with fear
Crazed with pain into delirium
In agonies beyond imagination
Frantic to receive deliverance – the soothing balm, the calm of death
and We, as good Samaritans, oblige
their wish becomes command, a verdict, vindication
[biblically sanctioned incantation:]
Break them with a rod of iron
(intoxicating frightful torture)
Dash them in pieces
(excruciating deadly pain)

We are the skilled satanic disciples –
Barbaric sweet and cruel and oh - so ruthless
we are -
Exquisitely refined
totally committed craftsmen

Yet still and ever eager students, and then some -

And aren't we proud!
We are the imaged signature of YOU

Claiming possession and inheritance
We are the judges of the earth
["Executive Outcomes"]
Executioners.
(wholly credible because insane
wholly certain because impossible)

Three strikes and out
A spick, two niggers and a kraut,
Traveling on intersegregated roads
Preaching and teaching and breaking your silly codes

Chinkyniggerwogspickdagos
Chitlinkrautgypsiegooks
(Drei Zigeuner sah ich einmal ...)**

Yet still and ever eager students, and then some -
And aren't we proud!
We are the imaged countersignature of YOU

V

YOU:
Fuck your game
We no longer play
WE refuse!! We shun Your name!

Generating jealousy and greed and fear,
Unleashing malicious pains and poisoned pleasures,
Indulging in orgasmic orgiastic ecstasies

Ripping intestines - the nightmares of white snakes:
And we build Churches?
And we Pray?

Take note:
Beware of what YOU taught!
We changed the rules.

Feed your voluptuous bloodthirsty lust, YOU
Insatiable baby killer
YOU!
Have us play Ji-Reh, Tawanna, Symphony
Have us rape neighbors, kill our kin
Light Twin Tower torches
Engrave Your alphabet? [A for Auschwitz
B for Biafra
C for Coventry
D for Dachau …Darfur…Dresden…
H for holocausts
N for Nanking, Nagasaki …
R for Rwanda
S for Somalia, Soudan, the Somme …]
Need we go on?
Proof of YOUR Magnanimity?, your Mercy?
Proof of YOUR presence?
And we proclaim and praise?
Prostrate?

Take heed!
Beware of what YOU taught!
We changed the rules.
We help your misfits, your failures (or dare you call them your achievements?
Your spitting images perhaps?
your spit?

You audacious arrogant, abominable, abhorrent piece of shit - YOU
[have YOU no shame, Sir, have YOU no decency?]
YOU

VI

Desperation
            Love rekindeling extinction
Are we unformed reflections of unredeemed potentialities?
            Unredeemed?
            Unredeemable?

Supreme and still forever and all ways
Taunting to tease and teasing to defy
                        stays,
beguiling, brilliant, beautiful and high,
                        Lucy
in the Sky with Diamonds.
            - For You to live, to love
                For us to love and die.
To live - to love - to die --

VII

Un wholly - holy whole
Exalted,
Completely unfinished
  Naturally artificial
            Despisingly adored
            Insufficiently sufficient
            Fully empty
            Contrived

All things
No nothing is nothing
Yes: -
Nothing is Nothing -
---:
Nothing Is

VIII

Comtesssa Ahvani, Sierra, Vixen Venessa
April, Shauna Morena, Spring,
(Or Brandy Baby, Sanji, Suzie Treasure,)
Cast into bitches conjuring,
Plying and playing for profit and pleasure
Us
three times three but always still:
embraced, unenviable trinity

Brianna, Leeza, Danielle
(Odette, Hermine, Lizawetha?
Good continental women.)
Service providers that work
(daily Daley Daley, – still!)
the Windy City
The City that works

And Anal Ashley throws a bash
(wink)
with Mistress Maxine as ceremony marionette
and grimreaperette enforcer of etiquette to
controlled substances:
White, Yellow, Chocolate.
Showers golden and brown; gfe and bareback
daty, dfk,
French cool geek Greek and Russian Hot and so.

And so?
So what!
And if?
And so if what if and so why not? –
Mingle and mix, snatch catch a quick fix turn Trix and shove Dick's
be merry, do April, lay June and take Carry,
kiss eat and drink
(wink wink)

Fly high
still and forever with Diamonds
Lucy, Lucy in the Sky
Nirvana

IX

Dust
Clay
Flesh

Essences - ephemeral and effervescent,
compounds assembled:
but: (zugleich und auch)***

bodies
without music –

bodies
without hope –

bodies
without love

X

flesh

    but clay
    but dust
    but nothing

Essences - ephemeral and effervescent,
Compounds: re disassembled:

Nothing -
Nothing

*and tomorrow we strike back
**three gypsies I once saw
***at the same time and also

MY GARDEN

If you have come to die, then
Why have you come into my garden?

My garden grows
grasses and weeds,
flowers like tulips and daffodils,
carnations, peonies, lilac and lavender
Yes, and also the majestic thistle along with the five pointed hemp

My garden takes
the warm rays of the sun
the soothing rain of clouds
the cool shade of trees
Yes, and also the brisk freshness of the air

My garden ExAmplar:
a mentoring host
a spacious glade
a safe haven
Yes, on earth and under a starry sky

PROTESTATION

I resent:
The circumstances of my birth
The time
The place
the reason

And I also resent
The constrictions of my life:
The needs
the ways
the forms

And I further resent, quite and as well:
The outcomes –
The voices
The words
The wastes

SHEHESHE HESHE

Sheheshe Heshe:

Shehesheheshe!
Brittany Zee
Come to, come,
See
And be.
And stay

AKKILA

Drawn into deserted landscape
at dawn
Under drifting clouds
Weaving dreams of destiny and desire
Prisomed into intensive beams of rays
Like fire
The sun –
Charred

Warden watching the world
Roaming the range
From the Big River
To the far ridges
From the Twin Teats through death's deserts
To the western shores
And back:
angel fire
river side
arcadia

Not resting
with burden and baggage
bending just so –
bowing,
not breaking -
ever.
Just so!

7 June 2010

PARLEZ PARLEZ PARLEZ

For Carolyn,
12 June 2011

Parlez Parlez Parlez
The parrot
    [whose name they swore was Ex Creant Sir Merde]
repeated some uncomely things

They blamed it on the Padre
Who constantly prayed to his god
Or so it seemed to them
While he still moved his lips

But then it could have merely been
The bitterness of betrayal,
The recognition of deceit
Or an anticipated unenviable legacy
For him as one of those who once had dared

And after the parrot then came the pug,
And after the pug the ferret
And after them the OWL -- and the lemurs

And finally the Jester
What after all was he to do?
Praise the performance?

REJUVENATING NIGHT

21 October
For you, tricie Latrice,
Thursday, 18 October 2018, when you left us

Rejuvenating Night!

Embraced by quintessential quiet,
Suffused in black crystal blinding Light.

We:
As once and then again – again and once again
In spacetime sans frontiers;

we

WHAT IS THE MATTER

It is not a matter of
begging.
We do not beg.

It is not a matter of
forgiving.
We do not forgive.

It is not a matter of
forgetting.
We do not forget.

It is not a matter of
loving.
We do not love.

It is not a matter of
caring.
We do not care.

It is not a matter of
disregarding.
We do not!

So do not ask:
What is the matter?
It is not a matter of matter.

WHAT THE WIND TOLD ME

What the East Wind Told me:
Learn to Listen
Listen
Learn
Listen

What the South Wind Told Me
Learn to learn
Learn to love
Learn to love to learn
Love

What the West Wind Told Me
Let Go

What the North Wind Told Me:
Pre Pare

CAUTIONARY COUNTER CANTABURY VERSES

I

BALLAD IN MEMORY OF A FORTUNATE LASS

Oh learned professor,
oh stubborn young fool
With no regulations, no guidelines, no rule:
A hole in the staircase
caused the loss of your cool

Oh misguided miscreant,
oh stubborn young fool
While riding a hobby horse (or was it an ass?)
A word in the stair case
caused withdrawal of a lass

near a hole in the staircase
the lass named one hobby horse, two donkeys, one ass
and to no one's surprise
pursues now her studies
at a college with style and with standards and class

II

DIRT FLOOR JUNGLE WARNINGS

[the provost's confession to resist all concession]

To all who would listen

I warn You:
Do not tease.
Please:
[Rikki-Tikki-Tavi listens up]

Shekena and Coach
It makes my blood boil
like a cobra I coil
When these subjects are mentioned
When these topics approach
I warn You:
Shove it,
Strip this bit of
arrogant offensive Ego trip,
[Rikki-Tikki-Tavi is not amused]

Listen to me:
If you want to stay then
Listen to me and do what I say;
Explicitly, implicitly, or ever which way
Get my permission:
Inform me,
Obey!
Do not do what I have not approved
What I have not allowed
What I have told you not to
Or else;
you will be removed
[Rikki-Tikki-Tavi becomes irritated]

As long as I live I remain in control
I set the tone
I dictate the protocol
I manage the money
I manage the people

If they need the job and intend to stay
They better fech, carry, and do what I say
[Rikki-Tikki-Tavi poises his whiskers]

Without my one offspring
With boredom no end and no other joy
This school is my one and my only,
        My thing
My pathological inclusive ego toy
[Rikki-Tikki-Tavi makes short shrift]

III

AND THEN FOR THE REST: AN ADMISSION REP'S RAP SONG

[A dean's lament – a disturbing litany, a testament of distress]

For you, Ho: HoHo

Let them take the average, the good,
The bright and the best
But we are the college that covets the money
And take all the others and welcome the rest
The ones who are bright – for whom college is right
At most stay one quarter and if not before
By then they take flight

But we: Oh yes and we do: we very much care
In sum:
We do our best to cajole and to snare
To beg and to bargain
with unfit, unwilling, the under-prepared
in short: with all of the rest
In our college there is always still space
And We are their school, we are their place

And yet: I tell you: 'Bet 'ya, you bet
no transcript, no GED?
No GPA, no ACT?
Say what? You have it? you don't? not yet?
F'ck it, no sh't. Well, let us see:
We'll still get you in – I tell you; you bet
And soon you will find that
we are, yes really we are, Your university
In so many words, in so many ways
no doubt and no question:
We are your place

Come one –
come all
Let's play college and let's have some fun
Starting whenever, yes, starting this fall.
We enforce our standards and that's easily done
Since - don't mind my saying so - we still have none.
Just sign, right here, on the thin dotted line
(you still can't quite write yet? Then just draw three crosses)
I will be witness, it's all right with my bosses

IV

HOW WELL WE REMEMBER

[a Chancellor's monologue – a chant of
reaffirmation for the formerly faithful]

PROLOGUE:

How well we remember
The Points of December
In all there were Five
But from now on 'till then

the Real question is:
How Will We Survive?

[chant of the Chorus Ebrius:]

Beware, oh, of hubris and ego and greed
Avoid white-out, starred courses, deceit,
Pound-foolishness, penny-wise ways,
Since all these will hasten
Disgrace, demise and defeat
Indeed:
Stay true to your mission. Hold on to your vision
Provide Service for all those in need.

I

Our alpha is admissions
Without alpha no omega
Strategic marketing tacticians
Fearless selling-skilled practicians
Theories and plans abound
Only numbers count
The real question is
How will We Survive?

[chant of the Chorus Ebrius:]
Indeed:
Stay true to your mission. Hold on to your vision
Provide Service for all those in need.

II

Retention is the second point we mention
students need our full attention.

play the friend, buffoon, sage, clown,
right side up or up side down,
beg, bargain, and promise the sky
appeal to their vanity, you clearly know why!
do it quick by treat or by trick
just be sure to make them stick

the Real question is:
How Will We Survive?

[chant of the Chorus Ebrius:]

Indeed:
Stay true to your mission. Hold on to your vision
Provide Service for all those in need.

III

And as to points three, four, and five:
Forget – do not remind, do not revive
While they make sense,
They are of little consequence
the Real question is:
How Will We Survive?
The answer for real:
To any all means we now appeal
For bare survival we strive

[chant of the Chorus Ebrius:]

Indeed:
Stay true to your mission. Hold on to your vision
Provide Service for all those in need.

IV

POST MORTUM
Caasiwan oh Jaadumane
From choosers to beggars,
From beggars to loosers,
Corroded through Ego
All means, all methods, all tricks, no despise
Used and worn out at the end all disguise.
        Do not follow their ways
        [a word from the wise]

[chant of the Chorus Ebrius:]

Beware, oh, of hubris and ego and greed
Avoided white-out, starred courses, deceit,
Pound-foolishness, penny-wise ways,
Since all these hastened
Disgrace and defeat and demise.

Indeed:
Had you stayed true to your mission,
Stayed upright and honest
held on to your vision
Provided true Service for all those in need.
        Surely no doubt you would have survived.

V

HOTCH – POTCH AND FOREVER

[22 July 2009:" You have authorized … for certificate …taken hotch-potch courses and not eligible…]"

This is the ballad of Hotch and Potch,
hotch-potch offsprings of hotch-potch parents

In a hotch-potch world
During a hotch-potch time

Once a time and long ago
Forlorn during a long hotch-potch night
when hotch-potch will grow –
There hotch-potch is born
with no traces of light
in a field full of thorn
    Masiwadu
    Masiwadu
Yes with no traces of light in a field full of thorn

Two hotch-potch parents had hotch-potch twins
And named them Hotch and Potch.
And Hotch and Potch the twins,
Grew up with all the other,
yes also hotchpotch-potchelings
    Masiwadu
    masiwadu
grew up with all the other, yes also hotchpotch-potchelings.

Made friends with hotch-potch fools
Hotch-potched in hotch-potch programs
At local hotch-potch schools
Were truely hotch-potch busy
with many hotch-potch tools
learned many hotch-potch thingies
and many a hotch-potch things
    Masiwadu
    Masiwadu
With many hotch-potch thingies and many a hotch-potch things

Took all the hotch-potch courses
Used all the hotch-potch sources

Did each its hotch-potch thing
At H-P U
At Hotch-Potch U
Their hotch-potch Uni-versity
[Ra Ra Hee Hee
He He See See,
Go hotch-potch hotch-potch hotch-potch,
GO Hotch-Potch Univer see tee!]
          Masiwadu
          Masiwadu
Go Hotch-Potch Uni-verse-e-t

And just before they closed their lids,
They gave the world more hotch-potch kids
the three initiatives:
First Sizzle, then Frazzle, then Fizzle
Just as their hotch-potch parents did
Some where some time and long ago
Hotch-potching hotch-potch
over and over - and always just so
Sizzle and Frazzle and Fizzle.
          Masiwadu
          Masiwadu
Yes, over and over and always just so:
First: Sizzle, then: Frazzle, last: Fizzle.

Now we have ended.
The ballad is true;
And if you enjoyed it,
May someone show mercy
For now and forever – and also to you
          Masima masima
             Masiwadu
For now and forever – and also to you

A MULE PARABLE

From a psydo-apocryphic text found in an as yet unauthenticated manuscript at an as yet unidentified place:

There once was a mule standing in the middle of a meadow. It was the most adorable, and lovable little mule that ever was. Once, so it was said, it had been a strong and healthy mule and highly regarded in all of muledom. But now it looked weak, sick, and emaciated. For ever so long the little mule had remained in one small area, consumed all natural edibles, used up all resources, and in one word, was stuck in a rut. Many a mule guide applied and accepted the challenge of caring for and nurturing the adorable little beast and to lead and guide it into green meadows and luscious pastures. But none succeeded to move the mule from its small area. They talked to the mule, scratched its ears, caressed its nostrils, stroked its back and its belly, pulled on its tassels in front and pulled on its tail in back, enticed it with carrots and sought for its attention by patting its rump. They tried sticks and stones, wheat and whip, push and shove, but the mule, as lovable, adorable, stubborn and proud a little beast it had ever and always been, remained just where it was. And every so often it balked and kicked, had spells of ill temper and even occasional meanness and finally indulged in self-inflicting pain and auto-mutilation. Its guides found no cure, became exhausted, discouraged, and ended up at their wit's ends and at the ends of their ropes. They came to be replaced with alarming regularity. Who was there who did not solicit a suggestion? Who was there who did not call for a diagnosis? Who was there who did not call for a solution? Who was there who did not sense the open secret, the obvious cause of this excruciating affliction? The ears heard it and the eyes saw it: The poor little mule remained a thoroughly confused and disoriented little mule. It had become its own worst enemy in its small and well-worn but safe and familiar ground. When it turned North, a part of it itched to run South; when it turned West, something pulled it into the Eastern direction; when it turned South, its feet backed up Northward; and when it completed the circle and turned to the East, its instinctive nature made it go West. And so it remained: round and round it went and round once more and again, confined and clinging to the spot which it had occupied beyond living memory. What in fact it needed and for what indeed it was searching, was deliverance; it needed and wanted and searched for an ever so gentle but ever so firm and experienced a hand of a guide and healer; a physician in fact, who would claim it as a patient, teach it how to revive, how to pull together, how to break the vicious circle and walk again, by nature and nurture, toward objectives, goals, and mission - a straight line with eyes clear and head erect, with confidence and courage, with optimism and all round with an air of being at one in the spirit and for the cause of the Lord.

A VOCATIONAL CREDO

Concerning Education

Formal education remains constantly question-dignifiable ("fragwuerdig"). Teaching subject content and assisting in character formation are actions needed throughout the educational process from pre-kindergarten through post-graduate school; the relative emphasis evolves from minimal subject content and maximal character formation in the earliest grades to its diametric opposite during post-graduate study. It remains of the utmost importance that interest, compassion, concern for the student, mutual and expressed highest respect between student and teacher, constantly be present. Face to Face, contact between student and teacher is still irreplaceable; other mechanical and technical equipments and devices have become essential supports, but remain supports only. Often the most profound impact a teacher has is the result of spontaneous acts of conduct, acts demonstrating quality of character. Relevant solid subject matter competency, of course, must be insisted upon as an aspect of technical training and vocational preparation for any position. The creative arts, the assistance in developing free, creative, imaginative expressions in an interdependent environment are central, especially in the earlier school years. It is critical to the arriving at and the retaining of a society quantitatively immense but based upon an acceptable fusion of freedom of the individual with the breathtaking scientific, technological (and organizational) changes [for instance in: biology, chemistry, physics, astronomy, medicine, communications]- a revolution in the middle of which we find ourselves at this very moment. If we fail in finding an acceptable form, a small technocratic oligarchy will control everyone else or we will endure some form of fundamentalist anarchy. Opportunities for us to "change the world" presently have never been better: the techno-scientific advances, lack of any substantive threat from a foreign power, the leadership position the United States still (but only still!) retains, the natural resources still (but only still!) at our disposal, the political process of formulating and implementing selected interests by chosen representatives, the still sufficient number of people who care for the improvement of society along democratic guidelines, all attest to the opportunities. But precisely because of some of these factors, we have become also more vulnerable. None can be taken for granted, all have to be earned by active, constant, and committed participation: learning/contemplating, acting/doing, teaching. Changes of conduct, alas, on the part of human beings towards themselves and towards others as individuals, towards others grouped as family, as local, regional, global community, are of grave concern. If the art of living together or at least tolerating each other (although: will that be enough?) eludes us, no other achievement will be of any acceptable use. We are still powerful enough and still rich enough to take the lead (as distinct from doing it all or doing it alone and our way) to arrive at a comprehensive policy which is consciously global and consciously based upon the capabilities and interests of all human beings on the basis of true mutual respect and true interdependency. Human beings teaching to the best of their abilities human being in need of education and learning - teaching with compassion and commitment, assisted by techno-communicative tools now available, might well make the decisive difference for the successful survival of all of us. Not every student will be at the head of the class, but each can achieve the full potential and make unique contributions within the framework of constructive interdependency to the immediate and to the global society - regardless of gender, ethnicity, religion, or any other classificatory distinction or label. There are no longer any excuses to delay action.

NECESSITY NOT A LUXURY

[A paper presented at the Second National Conference on Enhancing Minority Attainment, 11-13 September 1992, Indiana University at Kokomo, Indiana.]

It is not so very long ago when I too made use of the irresponsible cliché which places the burden for failure of college students on the shoulders of the high school teachers who, in turn, lose no time to accuse the elementary school staff, who quickly point the finger at the parents who immediately find grave faults with the entire school system, the environment, and the new generation.

… I like to share some practical information and experience….

It is critical for program success that it receives the support of the entire site personnel.

Some examples:

Primary School D: This site was the most interesting in several respects and was perhaps the most instructive experience. Our program included 7 seventh graders and

13 eighth graders. The school is located in an area known for its unusually high drug presence. The rear alley, for example, is known as drug alley and a number of students are directly involved as consumers and as suppliers. …

Based on our experience so far we tentatively suggest the following three points:

A. that involvement at the grade school level is extended to cover grades 6 through 8, not just 7 and 8; …

C. that the area colleges and universities, especially those with degree program education departments, be directly involved and in fact engage in school adoptions a concept not all that new …

By choice we have targeted the highest homicide rate area in Chicago: the Englewood neighborhood. …

Example high school site A: According to the retention officer, the school at the moment straddles the fuzzy demarcation line of two gang territories. The school literally finds itself in a quasi no-man's land war zone. Students have been killed near the school as well as on school grounds; …

Example; High School site B: This high school is a school with a national athletic program and a corresponding reputation. In fact, it seems that most publicity – both positive and negative – is connected in some way to their former national championship and the bid for another one in the future….

The news coverages ended with a follow-up story of what happens to many of these initially so ardently, so unscrupulously, even shamelessly courted scholarship athletes in the college world:

Academically often underprepared, they soon find themselves on academic probation, suspension, then drop out, after which many drift around and sooner or later quit college altogether. …

Example: High School C: C is the area high school for elementary school site C. Most clearly in this case were we able to illustrate the need for across-the-board coordination….

Among some observations I would like to present the following:

1) Generally speaking … staff and faculty of a university working with a school – or anyone else for that matter – should

be ever so careful not to display an attitude; an attitude of arrogance and superiority …

2) … We need to leave behind us any form of artificial rankings or pecking orders; we need to listen closely to each other; we need to focus on the common goal of further developing, refining, delivering effective comprehensive education to individuals, and exclude any heterogeneous considerations and silly notions.
3) … programs imposed from above have a high failure and a correspondingly low achievement rate. … resources should be given to the local area organizations who substantively represent the concerns and interests and who reflect the composition of the local community….
4) … each school must remain in charge of determining the priorities and of setting the general tone. Program personnel must always be aware of the fact that they supplement, assist, strengthen, but never replace …
5) At the present time there are in operation a variety of federal, state, and local assistance programs,… But nevertheless I consider my following point here as still valid: Many programs are either too narrowly focused or they are too broad in scope; …
6) … decreasing class size drastically – which, by the way, is my suggestion to improve dramatically and immediately school performance at all levels, provided these are staffed with competent staff …
7) Do not promise more than you can adequately deliver'
8) … the sponsors and/or funding agencies should continue to monitor very closely the administration of their programs in substance, but at the same time give a rather broad latitude with regard to the specific application. …

   Let me briefly summarize and conclude:

   1) Schools and programs … must work in close cooperation with all educational institutions at all levels …

2) Programs … need to be further encouraged, expanded, and strengthened. This goal can be achieved without exorbitant financial expenditures although adequate financial support is a critical factor.
3) Dedication and commitment to and concern of and care for all persons involved in these programs, concretely documented by action, transcend whatever barriers exist – as a result of color, culture, location, or whatever….

Thank you.

J. ALDEN NICHOLS

28 June 2014

Well, so where is one to begin?

According to brief references printed by his publishers (Harvard, University of Illinois, Dorsey) J. Alden Nichols was born in Westerly, R.I. in 1919, graduated from Wesleyan University, obtained his M.A. and PhD. from Columbia University, held a Ford Foundation faculty fellowship and was a Fulbright scholar in Germany. He was a member of the American Historical Association and a founding member of the National History Center. He taught at Wesleyan, Skidmore, was a managing editor for Daedalus, Social Sciences and Humanities editor for the College Department of Ginn & Co., and then spent most of his time at the University of Illinois, where this graduate student first met him in the spring of 1962.

Perhaps the reflections of this graduate student may be too detailed and trivial for some, perhaps not professionally distanced enough for others, perhaps too eclectic and impressionistic for yet a third group. But then it is presented as it is because it portrays aspects of the J. Alden Nichols this graduate student has known since 1962: the person, the historian, the teacher: aware, sensitive, nuanced, judicious, humane, impacting unobtrusively, consistently, insistently, ultimately: wise. All who are interested enough to visit these pages (and it is an obituary, not an encyclopaedia entry) will at least not object, and hopefully appreciate these shared details. It is especially written with those in mind who retain J. Alden as a constant companion in their daily professional lives.

J. Alden's contribution to Interpreting European History, (vol. II, From Metternich to the Present) edited by Brison D. Gooch, published by The Dorsey Press in 1967, consisted of chapter 9, Bismarck. His presentation choices are indicative: a selection from the undeservedly neglected historian and brilliant stylist Erich Marcks (whose biographical treatment of the early Bismarck, according to J. Alden, "has remained the most sensitive and profound biographical volume" on Bismarck's youth); a selection from the 1965 Bundestag address by Hans Rothfels, (one of the most influential German post-World War II historians, Meinecke student, national, conservative and until recently with categorically impeccable anti-Nazi credentials); the liberal journalist, financier, and politician Ludwig Bamberger (exemplary and quintessential liberal Bismarck-admiring Bismarck critic); and the American historian Otto Pflanze,(representing, so J. Alden, "the most recent, readable, and judicious treatment that we have".)

The German texts have been skillfully rendered into finely nuanced English by J. Alden, preserving the original intent and atmosphere as much as generally translations as such allow, and, in the case of Hans Rothfels, indicates a footnote: "with author's corrections." The selections deliberately aim to "mix the permanent, basic, almost classic clash of opinions with the change in historical perspective" and the end of his introductory comments brings him back, as he says, "to my original point: since even heroic genius is human, it is well not to go too far in worshipping it." The Bismarck headings underscore this selection criterion: Faustian Hero; Founder of a Cult; Historical Disaster; Responsible Realist.

Scholars, especially those who focus on modern German history, have always respected highly J. Alden's two monographs on <u>Germany After Bismarck: The Caprivi Era</u> (Harvard, 1958) and the <u>Year of the Three Kaisers: Bismarck and the German Succession, 1887-88</u> (University of Illinois, 1987). Both have well stood the test of time, both have well resisted the never- ending updating of source materials (especially by eager and ambitious PhD candidates); both are still often included in bibliographies; both are a sterling model of combining what some readers might consider boring and methodologically dated political history with exemplary original scholarship and brilliance of style; both continue to be highly instructive and a pure pleasure to read.

His first publication he called Germany After Bismarck [and rightly so: certainly after 1890 and arguably after 1848, there never was a Germany Without Bismarck]; his projected next book was to focus on Bismarck in retirement; but the more he became engaged with the subject (during which time this graduate student was his research assistant), the more did he convince himself that it needed a preface, and so this preface became the monograph on the Year of the Three Kaisers – of course another Bismarck book. When he returned to the post 1890 project, other considerations intervened, last but not least the paucity of relevant sources, not allowing the telling of a sufficiently solid source-founded story, to meet his professional standards. ["the sources simply were not there (the Bismarck archive) Suddenly – with Wm. II's accession they stop – nothing. And the key … political sources are also lacking."]

Unlike the historian Erich Marcks, referred to above, with whom he shares in more than one way style and insight, J. Alden refused, resisted, remained an acutely aware Calvinistic critic (shades of Bamberger – mentioned above as well) – one of those who in their own way contributed elegantly and insistently to the safeguarding of human dignity and freedom from all attempts to impose any form of authoritarian restrictions. J. Alden wrote: "I think it is probably my Protestant upbringing – more Calvinist than Lutheran – that has made me so leery of fanaticism. That plus growing up in the 30s. It is not for nothing that I have Holbein's Erasmus on my office wall." Symbolic, this expressed attitude and atmosphere was embedded in every aspect of his teaching and mentoring.

As a matter of fact, looking at J. Alden's professional endeavors in their entirety, it turns out to be one long, sustained, polyphonic encounter and increasing fascination with Bismarck ["the Old man grows on you"] This fascination with Bismarck, with Bismarck's ambivalence ultimately concerning religion, historical development, the role assumed/assigned to human individuals therein, predestination, luck… it remained a thread throughout J. Alden study and teaching. Considering the content of his lectures interweaving romantic idealisms and romantic quests in its so many manifestations, including the music of Wagner, Debussy, Ravel, Mahler it may well be that J. Alden restricted his academic research to political history as a conscious and self-imposed strategy to contain his, as he himself described it, "own strong Romantic Idealism. I know its dangers first hand."

His graduate student recalls: HS 410 seminar, February 1962 [Topic: Congress of Vienna, Liberalism, Nationalism and Revolution, Statesmanship in the 1860s, Socialism] The pages of the student papers are filled with corrections, suggested stylistic and substantive improvements, critical evaluative comments – often over 15 per page! A range from "brilliant", to "you might have consulted with profit", to "fundamentally flawed" is representative commentary. There were no concessions in matters of quality, but and always with sympathetic support and for improvement.

Or take the delightful episode when his graduate student's fiancé enrolled into a reading course in German history and he asked him to suggest the readings for her.

His graduate student recalls: J. Alden drove hundreds of miles to attend the wedding of his graduate student; he drove hundreds of miles to participate in a seminar chaired by this his (former) graduate student; also shared funeral services. He freely exchanged archival evidences, and dug up bibliographical references (on Angkor no less, for example). Such and so much more exemplified J. Alden's never-ending expressions of concern, commitment, support, reassurance, encouragement, and praise, appreciation, and the joy in the success of his former students.

His graduate student recalls: He considered suicide (by one of his students) an act of irresponsibility not to be condoned or sentimentalized; he shared advice handed down in his family: "Beware of fathers that dress like mothers"; he found that young German Deutscher Akademischer Austausch Dienst(DAAD) applicants which he screened, as tending to lack self- confidence, while American Ford and Fulbright applicants tended to be over-confident; he was not overly impressed with the German Grosse Koalition because he feared for the life of a healthy political opposition.

His advice, when given, based upon astute observation grounded in acute psychological insight, was always thoughtful; J. Alden never did anything thoughtlessly. His suggestions went way beyond the class room office hour dimensions. As a random sample from so many others: to this graduate student he recommended to view the films Zorba The Greek (1964); Georgy Girl (1966); La Dolce Vita (1960); The 8th Day of the Week (1958); and, most impacting: The Pawnbroker (1964)

As to his research assistants: J. Alden avoided the common abuses. He was not less demanding for all that but never lost sight of the fact that assistants were in fact graduate students under pressure to complete their dissertations. And he protected his graduate students and PhD candidates from the adversities of intra-departmental politics and tensions. Knowing that this graduate student would be teaching someday, he "suggested" becoming his teaching assistant, dismissing any and all objections.

J. Alden did appreciate spontaneous student comments and was obviously touched and pleased by such as the one of a bright and unconventional mid-60s free spirit thanking him for a "cool course". Indeed, he loved conversation, with most everybody about most anything (including students, colleagues, assignments, work, politics, personal and personnel, departmental and institutional matters and such like) and these were always delightful, instructive, wise; there was never even so much as a hint of contrivance, artificiality, false or forced tone, let alone gossip, negativity.

Ah, and his family dog: during this graduate student's time it was Muffy.

He was not spared deepest grief – the loss of his wife, and his son (about which this graduate student did not then know).

In intensely personal matters J. Alden always retained a "vornehme Zurueckhaltung", a dignified reserve and he appreciated and respected its mutual observation.

Reading the obituaries, especially in the Historische Zeitschrift and the American Historical Association Perspectives, testimonials to extraordinary historians are not absent. And indeed, in the recent issue of the Perspectives there is a fine example of James Sheehan's reflective obituary for Hans-Ulrich Wehler (a nephew of a very good friend of the family of this graduate student since the early 1950s) who closed his eyes in July 2014, as did J. Alden Nichols on 28 June. (what month, and what day, what anniversary year for historians of modern Germany!).

But then:
Relative to overall attitudes, conduct, - at least in the way this graduate student understood them then - concerning history and matters of history, but also concerning matters of critical-sympathetic form in search for understanding and values J. Alden's impact on all of his students was profound, - certainly on this graduate student – and so was his exceptional, incomparable genteelness of manner and style: frank, open, thoughtful, sharing, with an indestructible and wonderfully optimistic, infectious, approach to, and outlook on, life.

These aspects seemed to touch students more than recourse to developing and postulating brilliant-stark controversies, bolstered by numerous publications and the reputation of an internationally known formidable knight in academic garbs (Taylor, Fischer). It always seemed to this graduate student that those internationally acclaimed historians needed to be studied assiduously and intensively, but then also needed to be ingested and digested, "overcome"; but in addition to that, J. Alden compelled to emulate, to embrace pedagogically and absorb without needing to be afraid of becoming someone other than oneself. No Namierites or Bielefeld schools forged in the image of a J. Alden would have been to his liking.

Countless facts and dates and names to which J. Alden first introduced his students may well have long since been forgotten or had to re-acquire on the way later; but not forgotten have they (and I do speak for them) the "Wertsetzungen", the careful selection of and nuanced presentation and demonstrated application of distinct values and norms - and while in and by itself not necessarily a scholarly shattering experience, yet as a whole an invaluable guiding into an atmosphere and sustained condition of the model historian, gentleman and mentor – [for those who attended: the atmosphere of Summer 1964 seminar discussions and debates, 4th floor Lincoln Hall, interrupted only by many long hours in the library – reading, thinking, reflecting, and then the urge to communicate as teacher and mentor.]

Eventually, so he wrote, "I have given up research and am enjoying literature and the intellectual stimulation of the NY Review of Books", having "lunch with the retirees (a large group [at the U. of Illinois]) once a month."; continuing as well his stays at his country retreat in Vermont, and the freedom of driving the automobile, at age 88 (and as long as possible thereafter).

The more this graduate student reflects over the years the stronger has become his conviction that he was fortunate indeed to have had such an exemplary mentor and guide. (How many read seriously much of Ranke now? of Droysen, Gardiner, Grote, Mommsen, Bury,

Trevelyan, Froude, McMaster, Channing, Meinecke? But the impact of a Meinecke as a Droysen and Sybel student on his students, and of these students on theirs, which is now practically our generation? the impact of Siegmund Neumann and Columbia professors on J. Alden...?.)

In the long run, the quantity of publications and public visibility is not nearly as significant as is the quality of character, impact of personality, and in service of and commitment to teaching, mentoring, guiding. And with regard to these qualities J. Alden surely has his place in that very select group of the best of the best; there is none better.

Well, so how is one to end?

Out there in the flat openness of Illinois surrounded by farms, pig pens, cattle barns, alfalfa and corn fields, it was a good, respectable, Department which J. Alden joined and remained a loyal member; among with others such as: Schroeder and Spence (his sometime office companion), Starr and Geanakoplos, Dawn, Erickson and Lee, Sirich, Graebner and Johannsen. Add to these Phillipson of the German department and Francis Wilson (paradoxically, for those who know) of Political Science – and indeed from Navy Pier (yes! Navy Pier): Stronks (English) Nicholson and Riddle (history).

The Department still IS - and on a special shelf of the ISNCE their publications are positioned next to each other (some uncomfortably so and not quite to their liking, surely, but then, it is the arrangement of THIS graduate student - for now) and who knows…

Ekkehard-Teja Wilke, U. of Illinois '62, MA,1963, Graduate student, Nichols PhD '67
Institute for the Study of Nineteenth Century Europe [ISNCE]
188 Lawton Road
Riverside, Ill., 60546-2357

DR.E

The study of history is an activity which may lead to inspired action and eventually perhaps to wisdom. It is not the only way but it focuses on us and in turn gives us focus and it is a good way.
Many persons connect history with a tradition of rhetoric; I do instead place it in the tradition of parrhesia, that is: an unreserved, total, commitment to and an obligation of being truthful [telling truth?] (from Foucault, but with different emphasis).

While fairly close to Johan Huizinga's definition ["History is the intellectual form in which a civilization renders account to itself of its past"] I would prefer my modified version: History is the formed communicative accounting based upon historical evidences, by someone of something to somebody.

In one of his letters to F. H. Jacobi (7 July 1793) Goethe referred to history as the most thankless and most dangerous discipline and therefor avoided "doing" history (most of the time). How much more difficult is it to attempt teaching history! No wonder:

Teaching history is a most difficult vocation demanding the highest degree of personal and public integrity, professionalism, and accountability. It combines Teaching (an activity that assists in developing the Good to full potential in addition to transmitting skills and techniques – or, as Heidegger puts it: teaching is allowing learning to take place) with History (an activity that arrives at rendering account, to use Huizinga's words, in addition to artificially extending – so Carl Becker - social memory).

It is ex emplare: a vocation that provides models, guidelines, standards, and norms; a vocation that provides a clearing for light and space to develop and to grow; and finally it provides a protective, demarcated circumference yet allowing for full range of intercommunication and interaction.

History teaching done right gives us the ground and fills us with content in context without which other professions that help us in time of need, may hardlyprovide permanent meaning.

’nit so ’limm
[get over it; pick up the pieces; and go on]

Nothing is nothing
[because everything, even nothing, is something]

Kai me amelesete
[give proper, adequate, attention to whatever you do]

ABOUT THE AUTHOR

Born in Pritzwalk, (Priegnitz), Germany to Elisabeth Kaufmann-Wilke and the later renowned Riverside-Brookfield German teacher Wilfried Otto Georg Wilke, the family came to the United States and settled in the Chicago area. His primary and gymnasia education E-T received in Germany and then obtained his bachelor's, masters, and doctorate degrees from the University of Illinois (Navy Pier and Champaign-Urbana), majoring in modern European history with minors in Education, political science, and German. At Indiana University Bloomington he also received a masters degree in library and information science.

His teaching experience extends from 1965 through the present, including a short time at the University of Illinois and then Indiana University (Kokomo) and East-West University. Teaching fields included German, world history, American history, history for secondary school teachers, and specialized seminars, both at the graduate and undergraduate levels.

Based upon the combination of training, experience and commitment, E-T's vocation and professional career has been and continues to be focused on post-secondary institutional tutoring, teaching, and educational administrating in an environment which allows for full assistance to individuals, especially disadvantaged and minority individuals, to achieve their potential within a framework of constructive interdependency.

Publications include a monograph on a German government crisis in the 1890s, (dissertation 1967; and as book: POLITICAL DECADENCE IN IMPERIAL GERMANY: Personnel-political aspects of the German Government Crisis 1894-97 (Urbana: University of Illinois Press, 1976). editorship of an academic journal focusing on European history, reviews in academic journals, and a national conference presentation on minority education: STUDIES IN MODERN EUROPEAN HISTORY AND CULTURE. 3 vols. (Riverside: 1975-79).

E-T founded and continues to be active as director of the Institute for the Study of Nineteenth Century History, (ISNCE) 188 Lawton Road, Riverside, Illinois, USA

CPSIA information can be obtained
at www.ICGtesting.com
Printed in the USA
BVHW071144270319
543848BV00005B/657/P